Did Jesus really die?

Or did someone else die in His place?

E.M. Hicham

Word of Hope
Ministries

Did Jesus really die?
Copyright © 2011 E.M. Hicham

Published by Word of Hope Ministries
PO Box 24, Rochdale OL16 3FB England
Email: contact@word-of-hope.net
Website: www.word-of-hope.net

British Library Cataloguing in Publication Data. A catalogue
record for this book is available from the British Library

ISBN: 978-1-908392-00-8

Design & Print Management by: www.printbridge.co.uk

How to read Bible references:

Matthew 24:35 = The Gospel according to Matthew, chapter 24, verse 35

Contents

Introduction

"We Muslims only regard Jesus Christ as a prophet, but we honour Him and God by believing that God delivered Him from the cross. Yet you Christians claim He was God's Son[1] and teach that God did nothing while they crucified Him. How can you expect us to believe this? God would never have allowed one of His prophets to die in such a way."

One Muslim took this argument further with my Christian friend. "How many sons do you have?" he asked. My friend replied, "Three". "Well," he said, "if you saw a mob attacking one of them and could see that they were going to kill him, wouldn't you go and rescue him? Don't you love your son?" I intervened and said to our Muslim friend, "Let me strengthen your argument before we answer your question. What if you saw my friend walking down the road with a knife in his right hand and his son in the other, intending to kill his son? Wouldn't that be worse?" He agreed. I continued, "Then how can you believe that Abraham was such a

---

[1] E.M. Hicham has written a booklet called, 'How can God have a Son?' Contact us if you'd like a free copy.

great prophet and father when that is precisely what he did. One day he made preparations to kill his own son, according to the Qur'an (Surah Al-Saffat 37:102-103). How can you think well of Abraham when he was prepared to kill his very own son?"

Our Muslim friend replied, "You don't understand. That was different! It was a test of Abraham's love for God. If a man will give his own son for God, he'll give anything for Him!" "Exactly," I replied, "and that is precisely what we are saying about God. He did not stand by watching indifferently, but willingly gave His Son for us to save us from our sins. It was the greatest proof of His love that He could have given." The Bible says that "God so loved the world that He gave His only begotten Son that whoever believes in Him should not perish but have everlasting life" (Bible, Injil, John 3:16). When God commanded Abraham to prove his love for God by sacrificing his son, God was giving a picture showing what He was going to do Himself because of His love for us. Christians know that through the cross God has given the very best for us. Does Islam have anything like this?

Regarding the statement: "God would never have allowed His prophet to die in such a way", I would like to remind my Muslim friends of some verses from the Qur'an that teach of messengers (prophets) of God who were killed:

"...In that they [the Jews] broke their covenant; that they rejected the signs of Allah; that they slew the Messengers in defiance of right..." (Qur'an, Surah 4:155)

"We gave Moses the Book and followed him up with a succession of apostles; We gave Jesus the son of Mary clear (signs) and strengthened him with the holy spirit. Is it that whenever there comes to you an apostle with what ye yourselves desire not, ye are puffed up with pride? Some ye called impostors, and others ye slay!" (Qur'an, Surah 2:87; also see Surah 2:91 and Surah 3:183)

The heart of the Christian faith

More than two billion people today all over the world base their faith on the historicity of the crucifixion and the resurrection of Jesus! The crucifixion, death, resurrection and future return of Jesus Christ are at the heart of the Christian faith. Everything a Christian believes in and hopes for revolves around Jesus' death on the cross for unworthy sinners. If it can be proved that Jesus did not die and rise from the dead, then Christianity is nothing more than a great lie which has deceived billions throughout the ages. The Christian is left without hope, having no assurance of salvation or of going to paradise. He remains in his sins. (Bible, Injil, 1 Corinthians 15:12-19; Romans 4:25; 5:8-11)

However, there is overwhelming historical and factual evidence that Jesus died on the cross and rose again on the third day. The evidence for Christ's death is greater than that for almost any other event in the ancient world. There are a multitude of New Testament manuscripts. The historicity of the Gospel records has been confirmed by contemporary eyewitnesses.

Good questions to ask

The most important questions to ask are: "Why was Jesus' death necessary?" "Why do Christians insist on His death?" "What is the point?" and "How can His death two thousand years ago affect me today?" These were the questions that I struggled with myself before I became a Christian. I couldn't see the point of Jesus' death until one day when I understood the answer as I read God's Holy Word – the Torah.

But before we look at those good questions, we are going to answer other questions, "Did Jesus really die?" "Is it a fact?" and "If it is, what is the evidence?" In science and investigative journalism, we pursue truth passionately. Why should it be different in this important realm?

Chapter 1

What did the prophets before Jesus say?

The death of Jesus is not an idea that Christians invented in the first century. Amazingly prophets hundreds of years before Jesus' time spoke about it.

When a disciple tried to prevent Jesus' crucifixion, Jesus rebuked him and said,

"Do you think that I cannot now pray to My Father, and He will provide Me with more than twelve legions of angels? But how then could the Scriptures be fulfilled that say it must happen in this way?" (Bible, Injil, Matthew 26:53-54)

Jesus was saying that His crucifixion was actually a long planned culmination of God's plan foretold in the previous Scriptures, meaning the Tawrat (Torah) , Zabur (Psalms), and Prophetic Writings.

The prophet Isaiah

For example, seven hundred years before Jesus' crucifixion, the prophet Isaiah foretold what the Messiah (al Masih) would do when He came. He wrote,

"Surely He [Christ] has borne our griefs and carried our sorrows; yet we esteemed Him stricken, smitten by God, and afflicted. But He was wounded for our transgressions; He was bruised for our iniquities. The chastisement for our peace was upon Him, and by His stripes we are healed. All we like sheep have gone astray; we have turned, every one, to his own way; and the LORD has laid on Him the iniquity of us all. He was oppressed and He was afflicted, yet He opened not His mouth; He was led as a lamb to the slaughter, and as a sheep before its shearers is silent, so He opened not His mouth. He was taken from prison and from judgment, and who will declare His generation? For He was cut off from the land of the living; for the transgressions of My people He was stricken. And they made His grave with the wicked— but with the rich at His death, because He had done no violence, nor was any deceit in His mouth." (Bible, Isaiah 53: 4-9).

This is a remarkable prophecy which tells us clearly, not only that the Messiah would die but also why He would die!

What do sceptical Jews do with this passage? Many of their commentators state that this is about the Messiah who has not yet come; others have tried to find other interpretations. The Jews do not even include this chapter in their religious readings these days, because it speaks so clearly of Jesus and reminds them that they have rejected the promised Messiah when they demanded His death.

It is also worth noting that although the Jews vehemently deny that Jesus is the Messiah and that He fulfilled these prophecies, they have never dared even once to tamper with their Holy Scriptures and cut these things out. If there was ever a passage in the Old Testament that the Jews might love to have changed or removed, it would have been this one (Isaiah 53). Yet it remains! God has protected His Holy Scriptures.[2]

Alex, a friend of mine, is Jewish. He told me that during all his visits to the synagogue, he never once heard a Rabbi read Isaiah 53. When Alex heard about the prophecies, he compared them with the record of the life of Jesus in the New Testament (Injil), and was astonished at what he discovered. For the first time he realised that Jesus must be the One mentioned and to whom the Jewish Scriptures pointed. He has been a follower of Jesus ever since.

The prophet David (Dawud)

The prophet David (1,000 years before Christ) also spoke of the death of Jesus. In one of the psalms (Zabur) he prophetically spoke of the piercing of His hands and feet; this obviously did not happen to David but to Christ when He was nailed to the cross. This is what he said, "My strength is dried up like a potsherd, and My tongue clings to My jaws; *You have brought Me to the dust of death.* For dogs have surrounded Me; the congregation of the

---

[2] E.M. Hicham has written a booklet called, 'Has the Bible been changed?' Contact us if you'd like a free copy.

wicked has enclosed Me. *They pierced My hands and My feet*; I can count all My bones. They look and stare at Me. They divide My garments among them, and for My clothing they cast lots." (Zabur, Psalm 22:15-18) History tells us that that is exactly what happened to Jesus when He was crucified!

The prophet Zechariah (Zakaria)

The prophet Zechariah, about 500 years before Christ came, referred to the piercing of His side with a spear (Bible, Zechariah 12:10), which a Roman soldier did to Christ to make sure that He was truly dead (Bible, Injil, John 19:28-30).

When we read the gospel accounts of how Jesus died, we are struck by how the prophets described everything in such detail, hundreds of years beforehand: His silence in the face of false accusations; the way He was "slaughtered" on our behalf; His death between criminals; the fact that His body was laid in a rich man's tomb; His pierced hands and feet; the stares of the crowd. The prophets even mentioned the soldiers who gambled for His clothes! Everything was fulfilled exactly as predicted, because the author of the Bible is God, who knows the end from the beginning.

Chapter 2

What did Jesus Himself say?

Jesus told His disciples in advance that He would die and rise again. Many passages could be cited, but the following quotations from the Gospels (Injil) should be enough.

"When Jesus came into the region of Caesarea Philippi, He asked His disciples, saying, 'Who do men say that I, the Son of Man, am?' So they said, 'Some say John the Baptist, some Elijah, and others Jeremiah or one of the prophets.' He said to them, 'But who do you say that I am?' Simon Peter answered and said, 'You are the Christ, the Son of the living God.' Jesus answered and said to him, 'Blessed are you, Simon Bar-Jonah, for flesh and blood has not revealed this to you, but My Father who is in heaven.'… From that time Jesus began to show to His disciples that He must go to Jerusalem, and suffer many things from the elders and chief priests and scribes, and *be killed*, and be raised the third day" (Bible, Injil, Matthew 16:13-17; 21) "Now while they were staying in Galilee, Jesus said to them, 'The Son of Man [a title Jesus often used for Himself] is about to be betrayed into the hands of men, and they will kill Him, and the third day He will be raised up.' And they were exceedingly sorrowful" (Bible, Injil, Matthew 17:22.23).

Then later, when He was going up to Jerusalem, He took His twelve disciples aside on the road and said to them,

"Behold, we are going up to Jerusalem, and the Son of Man will be betrayed to the chief priests and to the scribes; and they will *condemn Him to death*, and deliver Him to the Gentiles to mock and to scourge and *to crucify*. And the third day He will rise again." (Bible, Injil, Matthew 20: 18, 19)

In addition, in this same chapter He tells them that this is why He came to this earth. He came not "to be served, but to serve, and to give His life a ransom for many." (Bible, Injil, Matthew 20:28)

We will see later the reason for Jesus' death. For now let us be clear that it was His mission to die on the cross. As He approached His crucifixion, He said, "Now My soul is troubled, and what shall I say? 'Father, save Me from this hour'? But for this purpose I came to this hour. Father, glorify Your name." (Bible, Injil, John 12:27)

It is obvious that the disciples did not make up the story of Jesus' death. In fact, they were devastated until they saw Him again after His resurrection. At that time He appeared to them on several occasions for a period of forty days proving to them that He physically rose from the dead. He also explained to them that His death and resurrection were a fulfilment of what was predicted in the Old Testament prophecies.

"This is what I told you while I was still with you: Everything must be fulfilled that is written about me in the Law of Moses, the Prophets and the Psalms." Then He opened their minds so they could understand the Scriptures. He told them, "This is what is written: The Christ will suffer and rise from the dead on the third day, and repentance and forgiveness of sins will be preached in His name to all nations, beginning at Jerusalem." (Bible, Injil, Luke 24:44-47)

Chapter 3

What did the apostles of Jesus say?

Jesus' death is directly mentioned more than one hundred and fifty times in the New Testament (Injil) alone. We can trust the Bible and what it says about Jesus' crucifixion because it records the testimony of eyewitnesses. The Bible chronicles what took place publicly. This is why for nearly two thousand years, all true followers of Christ throughout the world have believed in the crucifixion, death and resurrection of Jesus Christ.

From the first day the apostles preached the death of Jesus for the forgiveness of sins. This was not something that they invented later. For example, seven weeks after Jesus' crucifixion, Peter said to a great multitude of the Jews: "Men of Israel, hear these words: Jesus of Nazareth, a Man attested by God to you by miracles, wonders, and signs which God did through Him in your midst, as you yourselves also know - Him, being delivered by the determined purpose and foreknowledge of God, you have taken by lawless hands, have crucified, and put to death; whom God raised up, having loosed the pains of death, because it was not possible that

He should be held by it." (Bible, Injil, Acts 2:22-24) Did the hearers deny Jesus' crucifixion? Never! In fact 3,000 of them put their trust in Jesus after Peter had finished speaking to them!

Later, the apostle Peter, speaking to the Jews after the healing of a crippled man, boldly stated, "Let it be known to you all, and to all the people of Israel, that by the name of Jesus Christ of Nazareth, whom you crucified, whom God raised from the dead, by Him this man stands here before you whole." (Bible, Injil, Acts 4:10)

The apostle Paul, writing to believers in Corinth, Greece, said, "Moreover, brethren, I declare to you the gospel [i.e. the good news] which I preached to you, which also you received and in which you stand, by which also you are saved, if you hold fast that word which I preached to you—unless you believed in vain. For I delivered to you first of all that which I also received: that Christ died for our sins according to the Scriptures, and that He was buried, and that He rose again the third day according to the Scriptures," (Bible, Injil, 1 Corinthians 15:1-4)

Did the disciples make up the story of Jesus' death? If the writers of the gospels had been inclined to exaggerate, they would have been restrained from doing so because a great many people were still living who had witnessed the events of which they were writing. Many were their enemies. If the disciples had included errors or exaggerations, they would have been challenged by people in a position to know what really happened. For this witness they were flogged and thrown into prison. Most of the apostles eventually died as martyrs for their faith in the crucified and risen Christ. Few people would willingly suffer torture and death for something they knew to be false because they invented it themselves.

Chapter 4

What did the Roman authorities say?

Jesus' injuries made His death unavoidable. He had no sleep the night before He was crucified. He was brutally beaten and whipped, and He collapsed while carrying His cross. This prelude to the crucifixion alone was life-draining. So let us be clear that Jesus was dead, dead beyond any shadow of doubt. He was certified as dead by the Roman centurion in charge of the execution squad. Pilate, the governor, double-checked to make sure Jesus was dead before he gave the body to be buried. "Pilate marvelled that He was already dead; and summoning the centurion, he asked him if He had been dead for some time. So when he found out from the centurion, he granted the body to Joseph" (Bible, Injil, Mark 15:44-45).

Chapter 5

What did the medical testimony say?

The crowning proof of Jesus' death is that, when a spear was thrust into His side under His heart in order to make sure He was dead, an eyewitness said that 'blood and water' came out (Bible, Injil, John 19:34f). Obviously the scientific explanation of this was unknown to men of those days, but the conclusion is clear. Dark blood and light serum came from the body of Jesus, and the separation of clot from serum in the blood is the strongest medical proof that a person is dead. So don't swallow any of the "swoon" theories which suggest that Jesus was not quite dead but recovered in the cool of the tomb! He didn't survive it as Ahmadiyya Muslims, or Ahmad Deedat and Zakir Naik[3] think. He was dead!

---

[3] Ahmad Deedat and Zakir Naik have recently popularized a Qadiani theory about Jesus' death called the "swoon theory". A hundred years ago, Mirza Ghulam Ahmad, the founder of the Ahmadiyya sect of Islam, introduced the swoon theory to the Muslim world - while also claiming that he himself was the promised Messiah, the Mahdi, and a 'subordinate prophet.' Deedat preached this Qadiani swoon theory in South Africa, but Sunni leaders and publications condemned Deedat's methods and opposed his swoon theory as a non-Muslim Qadiani theory. While Deedat has gradually lost his credibility among Muslims in South Africa, his disciple Zakir Naik has revived Deedat's theories in South Asia. Naik also has been condemned by Islamic scholars such as Darul Ifta of the Darul Uloom Deoband (India's foremost Islamic centre of theological learning).

Chapter 6

What did early Christians say?

The earliest Christian writers after the time of Jesus (called, the early fathers of the church) affirmed His death on the cross by crucifixion.

Polycarp, a disciple of the apostle John who had watched the crucifixion, repeatedly referred to the death of Jesus, speaking, for example, of "our Lord Jesus Christ, who for our sins suffered even unto death". Ignatius (AD. 30-107), a friend of Polycarp, wrote, "And He [Jesus] really suffered and died, and rose again. Otherwise," he added, "all His apostles who suffered for this belief, died in vain. But (in truth) none of these sufferings were in vain; for the Lord [Jesus] was really crucified by the ungodly."

Chapter 7

What do the practices of early Christians say?

In addition to the writings of the early church fathers we have already discussed, early church history and archaeology can be examined. This would provide more significant evidence of the beliefs of the first century Christians about the crucifixion, death and resurrection of Jesus. Drawings and inscriptions of the cross can be seen in the catacombs and vaults of Rome. These underground locations were the secret meeting places where early Christians gathered together to worship, away from the surveillance of the government's spies.

Early Christians also began to engrave the emblem of the cross on their tombs to distinguish them from the pagans' tombs. Remember, some of those martyrs were eyewitnesses of the crucifixion. Had these Christians not been sure of Christ's crucifixion they would never have adopted the cross as their emblem. Though the cross was a symbol of shame to both the Jews and the Romans, after the crucifixion of the righteous Christ it became a symbol of hope and faith to the Christians.

The ordinances of the Lord's Supper and Baptism are also historical evidence of Christ's death and resurrection. On the night in which Judas Iscariot betrayed Jesus, He Himself instituted this first ordinance and requested His disciples to continue it in His memory.

> "The Lord Jesus on the same night in which He was betrayed took bread; and when He had given thanks, He broke it and said, "Take, eat; this is My body which is broken for you; do this in remembrance of Me." In the same manner He also took the cup after supper, saying, "This cup is the new covenant in My blood. This do, as often as you drink it, in remembrance of Me." For as often as you eat this bread and drink this cup, you proclaim the Lord's death till He comes." (Injil, 1 Corinthians 11:23-26. See also Matthew 26:26)

Since then the Lord's Supper has occupied an important place in the practices of the church through the ages. The real significance of this ordinance, as Christ interpreted it, is that it is a symbol of His crucifixion and death. When Christians celebrate this ordinance, they always commemorate His death.

The same thing could be said about the ordinance of Baptism. It is a symbol of the Christian's death to the old life and resurrection with Jesus Christ. These two ordinances were practised by the disciples in compliance with Christ's commandment and are still practised by the church until this very day. If the crucifixion of Jesus was not a fact deeply-rooted in the faith of these Christians, they would not have practised these two ordinances.

Chapter 8

What did secular historians say?

Secular history also confirms the crucifixion of Jesus. There are extensive writings by non-Christians since the time of Christ that have discussed Jesus and His crucifixion as an historical fact.

Consider for example the first century Jewish historian, Flavius Josephus (AD 37-100). He lived in the area of Jerusalem where he gained access to first hand information. He documented the Jewish history and tradition for Rome.[4] With no ties to the Christians and no reason to fabricate his records to confirm the Bible account, Josephus wrote:

"Now, there was about this time, Jesus, a wise man, if it be lawful to call him a man, for he was a doer of wonderful works … a teacher of such men as receive the truth with pleasure. He drew over to him both many of the Jews, and many of the Gentiles. He was the Christ; and when Pilate, at the suggestion of the principle men amongst us, had condemned him to the

---

[4] Flavius Josephus, The Complete Works of Josephus, VI-IX, Antiquities of the Jews, Book XVIII, chapter III, Section 3.

cross, those that loved him at the first did not forsake him, for he appeared to them alive again the third day, as the divine prophets had foretold these ... and the tribe of Christians, so named from him, are not extinct at this day."[5]

The second-century Greek writer, Lucian, commented derisively on Christ and Christians. He failed to comprehend the true nature of the Christian faith. He could not understand the readiness of Christians to die for the sake of their beliefs. He regarded them as deluded people who yearned for the hereafter instead of enjoying the pleasures of the present world. He wrote:

"The Christians, you know, worship a man to this day -- the distinguished personage who introduced their novel rites, and was crucified on that account...and then it was impressed on them by their original law-giver that they are all brothers, from the moment they are converted, and deny the gods of Greece, and worship the crucified sage, and live after his laws."[6]

The letter of Mara Bar-Serapion (ca. AD 73), housed in the British Museum, speaks of Christ's death, asking: "What advantage did the Jews gain from executing their wise King?"[7]

There was also a Roman writer, Phlegon, who spoke of Christ's

---

[5] Ibid, 379.

[6] Lucian, The Death of Peregrine, p.11-13, in the works of Lucian of Samosata, trans, by H.W. Fowler and F.G. Fowler, 4vols. (Oxford: The Clarendon Press,1949), vol. 4, as quoted by Habermas, inThe Verdict of History, p. 100.

[7] Habermas, Gary R The Verdict of History,p 101, see also F.F. Bruce, The Origin of Christianity, p. 30.

death and resurrection in his Chronicles, saying, "Jesus, while alive, was of no assistance to himself, but that he arose after death, and exhibited the marks of his punishment, and showed how his hands had been pierced by nails."

Cornelius Tacitus (ca. AD 55-120), was the greatest first century historian of the Roman Empire. In his two major historical works, Tacitus recorded three references to Christ and Christianity. The most important one is found in his Annals[8]. He wrote, "The name Christian is derived from Christ, who was executed under the government of the procurator Pilate."

We have here strong, non-biblical evidence that Jesus did die! The crucifixion of Jesus is a well-attested event in history. Modern historians agree that Jesus was crucified. Even one of the acclaimed Muslim writers on the history of Egypt, Abbas Mahmood Al-Akkad (who lived in the 19th century), confirmed, in a book he wrote about Him[9], that we can depend on the four gospel accounts we have in the Bible (the books of Matthew, Mark, Luke and John) as historical evidence for what happened in Jesus' life.

If you want to seriously inquire more about the historical evidence for the life and death of Jesus, I recommend the following book: *The Historical Jesus, Ancient Evidences for the Life of Christ Gary R. Habermas, College Press Publishing Company, Joplin, Missouri, 1996; ISBN 978-0-89900-732-8*

---

[8] Habermas, Gary R. The Verdict of History, pp. 87-88; Thomas Nelson, Nashville, 1982.
[9] Al-Akad Abaas Mahmood, The Genius of Christ, Dar Al-Ahlal.

Chapter 9

What does the Qur'an say?

For Christians the Qur'an is not from God and therefore not authoritative, so strictly speaking what it claims would change nothing. However, Muslims claim it is from God and that it denies the death of Jesus. I would like to ask them whether that is necessarily the case.

Surah An-Nisa' 4:157-158

Ninety percent of the time, my Muslim friends will immediately quote, "They killed him not, they crucified him not, but it was likened unto them [or it appeared into them]. They killed him not knowingly, but God raised him and God is the most merciful of merciful." (Qur'an, Surah 4:157-158) In their minds, this verse says that God would never have allowed a great prophet like Jesus to be crucified by His enemies.

But does this verse really say that Jesus did not die? Is that how most Muslim scholars themselves interpret it? What does, "They killed him not knowingly," mean? The fact of the matter is that there are different contradicting interpretations of this verse amongst Muslim scholars.

There are various ways of interpreting Surah 4:157-158. One of them would be to remember the Jews' attitude toward Christ. When Jesus was taken to the Roman governor, they did not believe He was the Messiah. They wanted to get rid of Him. By saying, "They killed him not knowingly," the Qur'an simply states that they killed Jesus without knowing He was the Messiah.

Another possible way to interpret the passage (Surah 4:157-158) is that the unbelieving Jews intended by the crucifixion of Jesus to shame Him in the eyes of the world. The death He would suffer would then destroy and invalidate His mission in the eyes of the world. However, the Jews failed to accomplish their goal. In fact, by the crucifixion, Jesus was glorified when God raised Him up to be with Him. He became the key figure of human history. Throughout the years countless people have turned to Jesus Christ. Jews, Arabs, Asians, Europeans and people from all other nationalities and classes of society have experienced the life changing power of Jesus' life, death and resurrection.

Conclusion? It is not possible – despite what people usually think – to reach a definite conclusion based on this single and ambiguous verse. Muslim scholars are unsure about the end of the life of Jesus on earth. They disagree about whether He died or was raised alive to heaven without dying. Any conclusion from Surah 4:157-158 asserting that Jesus did not die involves speculation and theory. In fact, there are other verses in the Qur'an which say that Jesus was killed.

Surah Maryam 19:33

In this verse, Jesus is reported to say: "Peace is on me the day I was born, the day that I die, and the day that I shall be raised up to life (again)!" (Qur'an, Surah Maryam 19:33).

وَالسلامُ عَلَيَّ يَوْمَ وُلِدتُّ وَيَوْمَ أَمُوتُ وَيَوْمَ أُبْعَثُ حَيًّا.

Muslim scholars, who believe that Jesus did not die, find themselves in a dilemma at verses like this one. Many of them attempt to respond by saying that this is a future event. Jesus will come back to this world some day to do many great and wonderful things, and then He will die.

However, we read almost an identical passage in Surah Maryam 19:15 about Yahya (John the Baptist): "So Peace on him [Yahya] the day he was born, the day that he dies, and the day that he will be raised up to life (again)!"

وَسلامٌ عَلَيْهِ (يَحْيَى) يَوْمَ وُلِدَ وَيَوْمَ يَمُوتُ وَيَوْمَ يُبْعَثُ حَيًّا.

Muslims recognize the fact that Yahya died and was buried. Abdullah Yusuf Ali comments on this passage[10]: "This is spoken as in the lifetime of Yahya. Peace of Allah's blessings were on him when he was born; they continue when he is about to die an unjust death at the hands of the tyrant; and they will be especially

---

[10] Abdullah Yusuf Ali, Footnote 2469

manifest at the Day of Judgement."

I don't know of any Muslim who would shift the death of Yahya (John the Baptist) to the future! All know that Yahya died. Therefore, following the plain meaning of the parallel verse, no one should shift the death of Jesus to the future. In fact there isn't a single verse in the Qur'an showing that Jesus will return to die. Yahya died; the parallel statement clearly shows that Jesus also died.

Surah Al-Imran 3:55 and Surah Al-Maida 5:116-117

Another Qur'anic passage that speaks of the death of Jesus is Surah Al-Imran 3:55: "Behold! Allah said: 'O Jesus! I will take thee to Me [Arabic: mutawaffeeka, meaning 'I will cause you to die'] and raise thee to Myself and clear thee (of the falsehoods) of those who blaspheme; I will make those who follow thee superior to those who reject faith, to the Day of Resurrection.'"

إِذْ قَالَ اللَّهُ يَا عِيسَىٰ إِنِّي مُتَوَفِّيكَ وَرَافِعُكَ إِلَيَّ وَمُطَهِّرُكَ مِنَ الَّذِينَ كَفَرُوا وَجَاعِلُ الَّذِينَ اتَّبَعُوكَ فَوْقَ الَّذِينَ كَفَرُوا إِلَىٰ يَوْمِ الْقِيَامَةِ.

Still another is: "I (Son of Mary) was a witness over them whilst I dwelt amongst them; when Thou didst take me up [Arabic: tawaffaitani, meaning, 'caused me to die'] Thou wast the Watcher over them, and Thou art a witness to all things." (Qur'an, Surah Al-Maida 5: 117).

فَلَمَّا تَوَفَّيْتَنِي كُنتَ أَنتَ الرَّقِيبَ عَلَيْهِمْ ۚ وَأَنتَ عَلَىٰ كُلِّ شَيْءٍ شَهِيدٌ

The Arabic expression tawaffaitani (translated: take me up) is explained by Dr. Mahmud Shaltut, one of the previous presidents of Al-Azhar University: "(It) is entitled in this verse to bear the meaning of ordinary death ... there is no way to interpret 'death' as occurring after his [Jesus] return from heaven...because the verse very clearly limits the connection of Jesus ... to his own people of his own day and the connection is not with the people living at the time when he returns."[11]

These Qur'anic texts show that Christ died, even though they do not discuss how His death took place. Were the Biblical and other historic records of Jesus' crucifixion untrue, we would expect the Qur'an to have many verses stating that Jesus did not die on the cross. The truth is that, in more than 6,000 Qur'anic verses, there is not a single one that clearly refutes Jesus' crucifixion.

---

[11] Muslim World, xxxiv, pp. 214 ff; as quoted by Parrinder. Geoffery, Jesus in the Qur'an, pp.115-116; Sheldon Press, London, 1965.

Chapter 10

What do many Islamic scholars say?

L et us see how some Islamic scholars explain the Qur'anic verses quoted in the previous chapter.

Al-Razy

Concerning the expression, "It appeared so to them," (Surah 4:157-159) the great jurisprudent Imam Al-Razy wrote in his book *Al-Razy exegesis [Tafsir]*, part 3, page 350:

"If it is permissible to say that Almighty God put the resemblance of a man on another, this will open the door for confusion, so if we see (Zaied), he may not be (Zaied), but the resemblance of (Zaied) was put on someone else!!! If a man married to (Fatima), he might not marry Fatima, but the resemblance of (Khadija) was put on Fatima, so he would marry Khadija instead of Fatima, thinking that she is Fatima."

Imam Al-Razy concluded by saying:

"If it is possible to put the resemblance of someone upon

someone else, so neither marriage, nor divorce, nor ownership
is authenticated anymore."

So Imam Al-Razy denies that the expression, "It appeared so to
them," means that someone else was made to resemble Christ.

بخصوص تعبير "**شبه لهم**" يقول *الإمام الرازي* في كتابه (تفسير
الرازي جزء3 ص 350):

"إن جاز أن يقال إن الله تعالى يلقى شبه إنسان على آخر فهذا يفتح
باب السفسطة. فلربما إذا رأينا (زيداً) فلعله ليس (بزيد) ولكن ألقى
شبه "زيد" على شخص آخر!! وإذا تزوج رجل (فاطمة)، فلعله لم
يتزوج (فاطمة) ولكن ألقي على (خديجة) شبه (فاطمة) فيتزوج
خديجة وهو يظن أنها فاطمة".

وخلص الإمام الرازي إلى حقيقة خطيرة فقال:
"لو جاز إلقاء شبه أحد على شخص آخر فعندئذ لا يبقى الزواج
ولا الطلاق ولا التملك موثوقاً به".

فالإمام الرازي يستبعد أن يكون المقصود من هذا التعبير "شبه لهم"
هو إلقاء شبه المسيح على إنسان آخر!!

Moreover, commenting on Surah Al-Imran 3:55, Imam Al-Razy
said, "Narrated ibn Abbas and Mohammed ibn Ishak: the meaning
of 'tawaffaitani - take you to me' is to let you die."[12]

Al-Razy also said, "Narrated Wahb: the Christ died for three
hours."[13]

---

[12] Al-Razy exegesis [Tafsir] part 2 page 457
[13] Ibid

And he continued, "Narrated ibn Ishak: he [*Jesus*] died for seven hours."[14]

Al-Syouty

Al-Syouty is another Muslim scholar who explained that, when Surah 3:55 refers to Jesus' death, it means a real one. He said in his book Al-Itqan (The Perfection) part 1, page 116: "Take you to me [mutawaffeeka] means put you to death"

Ibn Kathir

Another famous Islamic annotator is Ibn Kathir. He wrote in his exegesis of the Qur'an *(tafsir al Qur'an)* that there are two different views of Surah Al-Imran 3:55 amongst Muslim scholars[15]. One of the two interpretations is that Jesus died a physical death.

Ibn Kathir said, "Narrated Ali ibn Abi Talha, narrated Ibn Abbas: the meaning of take you to me [mutawaffeeka] is to let you die."

He also said, "Narrated Mohammad ibn Ishak, Narrated Wahb: Allah let him die for three hours and then raised him."

Again he said, "Narrated ibn Ishak: Christians claim that Allah let him die for seven hours then he brought him to life again."

And again, "Narrated Ishak ibn Bashr, narrated Idriss, narrated Wahb: Allah let him die for three days and then he raised him up."

---

[14] Al-Razy exegesis [Tafsir] part 2 page 457
[15] Ibn Kathir, Tafsir Al Qur'an (Arabic text), Volume I, Part II, page 27-28 (my own English translation)

تفسير ابن كثير للآية : *إِذْ قَالَ اللَّهُ يَا عِيسَى إِنِّي مُتَوَفِّيكَ وَرَافِعُكَ إِلَيَّ وَمُطَهِّرُكَ* " (آل عمران 55) :

اختلف المفسرون في قوله: (*إِنِّي مُتَوَفِّيكَ وَرَافِعُكَ إِلَيَّ*) فقال قتادة وغيره: هذا من المقدم والمؤخر، تقديره: إني رافعك إلي ومتوفيك، يعني بعد ذلك.

وقال علي بن أبي طلحة عن ابن عباس: (*إِنِّي مُتَوَفِّيكَ*) أي: مميتك.

وقال محمد بن إسحاق، عمن لا يتهم، عن وَهْب بن مُنَبِّه، قال: توفاه الله ثلاث ساعات من النهار حين رفعه الله إليه.

قال ابن إسحاق: والنصارى يزعمون أن الله توفاه سبع ساعات ثم أحياه.

وقال إسحاق بن بشر عن إدريس، عن وهب: أماته الله ثلاثة أيام، ثم بعثه، ثم رفعه.

Although Arabic is my mother language and though I have read the Qur'an many times, I am not an expert in the interpretation of the Qur'an. However, I have tried to show that *not all Muslim scholars deny the death of Jesus (as you may think)!* The Qur'an contains very little material about what actually happened. There are quite a few question marks over the real meaning of the above verses. So, there is extensive contradiction and confusion in what Muslim scholars have to say about the death of Christ. Some have denied the death completely, and explained it as sleeping or death from having lusts; others have accepted the death but differed in their understanding of its duration: three hours, seven hours or three days! Therefore, if you are to know the truth, you need to be open-minded and look somewhere else – at extra-Qur'anic evidence. That is precisely the reason for this booklet!

Chapter 11

Did someone else die in Jesus' place?

Let us now spend some time looking at the Muslim theory of substitution. Often my Muslim friends tell me, "Jesus was taken up to heaven by Allah, before they could kill Him. He was not crucified. A person who looked like Him (Shabih) was put in place of Him by Allah, and the people thought it was Jesus. Glory be to God, the all-powerful, all-wise."

Think about it!

- I am truly mystified: How would a fake crucifixion bring any glory to God, especially if nobody knew about it until 600 years later at the time of Muhammad?

- If God really wanted to rescue His prophet, why didn't He just lift him up to heaven in full view of everyone? It would have been even more wonderful for people to see with their own eyes what God was doing, and see God's "vindication"! Why did He have to do it secretly? Why did He have to give someone else (innocent!) to the Jews to crucify? It makes no sense.

- God would not deceive people by making them think that it was Jesus whom they were crucifying, when in fact it was someone else. God doesn't lie!
- Would God allow the foundation of the Christian faith to be based on a deception and misidentification that He Himself had orchestrated? If so, it would make God the biggest hoaxer in human history. This cannot be; He is a just and holy God who always does what is right.

Now, I know that you, my Muslim friend, think that it would be a defeat if a prophet were killed at the hand of his enemies. For this reason, I'd like to ask you three questions:

First, which of the following would be a greater act by God? Which one of these would best show God's mighty power?

1. To deceive people and snatch Jesus up without letting Him die..., or,

2. To let Jesus die and then raise Him from the dead.

Raising someone from the dead is surely the greater act. So whereas Muslims say that Allah is so great that he wouldn't allow his prophet to die, Christians say, "Well, our God showed ever greater power by raising Jesus from the dead."

Secondly, which is the greater victory?

1. To escape death by allowing someone else to die in your place..., or,

---

[16] Ibid

2. To defeat death, by dying for others and rising from the dead? Surely the second option.

Here is my third question. Which of the following would best honour Jesus and bring most glory to God?

1. For Jesus to use violence to attack the people that were arresting Him,

2. For Jesus to escape..., or,

3. For Jesus, out of love for His enemies, to take the worst that they could inflict on Him (death on the cross), and then for Him to publicly conquer death by rising from the grave.

Obviously the third action would bring the most glory to God, and that is exactly what the Bible says that Jesus did.

The eyewitnesses

Let us return to the scene of the cross and question the eyewitnesses:

1. Could not the crucified substitute complain loudly and vigorously during his public trial that he was not Jesus?

2. The apostle John was so near Jesus at the time of His death that he saw blood and water flow out of the wound in Jesus' side (Bible, Injil, John 19:33-37). John knew Jesus intimately and would certainly have noticed if the crucified man was somebody else! Those who were present, like John, testify to Christ's crucifixion. Those who deny it were born hundreds of years afterwards and cannot therefore be accepted as witnesses.

3. How could Mary, the mother of Jesus, not see such a fraud as she stood at the foot of the cross and heard His voice speak lovingly to her? Nobody would know Jesus better than His own mother. What kind of God would allow Mary and the beloved friends of Jesus to suffer as they watched the agony of one whom they thought to be Jesus? Would God allow His followers to go through this tortuous experience because of an illusion that He Himself had orchestrated?

4. The centurion was a professional soldier. He would not mess things up nor allow anyone but the one delivered to him by Pontius Pilate to be crucified. That same professional executioner later confessed faith in Jesus because Jesus exhibited such holiness. A sinful traitor like Judas would never have left such an impression.

5. The gospel accounts (Injil) record seven statements that Jesus made while on the cross. No one else could have said such remarkable words. For example, how could anyone other than Jesus pray (while He was going through excruciating pain) that God would forgive His persecutors? How could such merciful and compassionate sentiments come from the lips of Judas, the traitor?

6. The criminal executed alongside Jesus would not have called on Him for salvation, nor would he have received salvation, if Jesus was just another sinner there on the cross beside him.

7. There is also another important issue that Muslim commentators failed to resolve: the case of Jesus' body. Muslims

claim that the substitute (Shabih) resembled Jesus in his face only. His body was not subject to any change. They said, "The face is the face of Jesus, but the body is not His body."[17] They made this statement in the context of their interpretation of Surah al-Nisa 4:157: "Those who are at variance concerning him [Jesus] surely are in doubt regarding him; they have no knowledge of him, except the following of surmise."

If this statement is true, how then did Mary fail to recognize the difference between the body of her son and the body of the crucified substitute? What about Joseph of Arimathea and Nicodemus, a member of the Sanhedrin and a secret believer in Jesus? In the context of the crucifixion story it is stated that they were able to obtain official permission from the Roman governor, Pontius Pilate, to lay Jesus in a tomb that Joseph had prepared for himself. If the crucified one was not Jesus, how did these two men fail to distinguish between Jesus' body and the body of an impostor? Did Judas have, for instance, the same height, weight and skin colour of Jesus? Did he have the same hair and other visible characteristics of his holy Master?

Furthermore, we learn that on the day of Jesus' resurrection, in the evening, He appeared to His disciples and said to them, "Peace be with you;" then He showed them His hands, where they

---

[17] Fakhradin Al-Razi: Al-Tafsir Al-Kabir p.102; vol. 11; Dar al Fikr, Beirut, Lebanon, 1981. Also refer to the Commentaries of the Jalalayn and the Baydawi concerning the interpretation of verse 157 of Surah 4.

could see the place of the nails, and His side, where He was pierced by the spear of the Roman soldier (Bible, Injil, John 20: 19-20). Thus He proved to them that He was the One who was crucified and that no-one had taken His place. These are tangible evidence that is hard for any objective researcher to overlook.

Besides, what would you think of God if for hundreds of years He had promised that Jesus would come to die for the sins of the world, and then, at the last moment, when Jesus was about to be put on the cross, He took Him alive and changed someone else to look like Him? Does this description fit God? Not only would this have made God out to be a liar, but there would have been no provision and satisfaction for man's sin! Jesus was the only sacrifice sufficient for man's salvation.

Chapter 12

So did Jesus really die?

I always ask my Muslim friends to provide me with reliable historical evidence that Jesus didn't die or that someone else took His place. So far none of them has given me an answer! That is not surprising because there isn't one! All the arguments point to the fact that there is no doubt, Jesus died!

In summary then, the evidence that Christ died on the cross includes:

- The prophets foretold the death of Jesus.
- Jesus Himself said in advance that He would die.
- The apostles of Jesus testify to His death.
- Pilate, the governor, certified Jesus' death.
- Dark blood and light serum came from the body of Jesus, and the separation of red cells from serum in the blood is a strong medical sign that someone is dead.
- Early Christians believed Jesus died.
- Archaeology and the practices of early Christians show that the crucifixion of Jesus was a fact deeply-rooted in their faith.

- Secular historians testify to the crucifixion.
- The Qur'an accepts Jesus' death.
- Many Islamic scholars accept Christ's death.
- It would have been impossible for someone else to die in His place. It has no historical proof.
- After His resurrection, Christ appeared to His disciples and told them why He died. He showed them the marks of His crucifixion, proving to them that He really was the One who had been crucified.

Can anyone seriously doubt Jesus' death?

Now we come to the most important question....

Chapter 13

Why was Jesus' death necessary anyway?

The death of Christ is not only a fact (with, as we have seen, much reliable evidence), it is also a very important fact. Why do Christians insist on His death? What is the point? Why did Christ need to die? If He is the Saviour, could He not have saved us without dying? These are very important questions. They are at the heart of the Christian faith. To find the answers, we must go back to the beginning, to creation. We need to grasp what happened in the Garden of Eden (جنة عدن).

How did it all begin?

Everything about the world that God made was good. There was plenty of food and drink for every living creature. It was in this lovely setting that the first people, Adam and Eve, lived. If they had continued to live for Him, obeying Him, they would have lived forever; but that if they disobeyed Him they would surely die. God commanded Adam, saying, "Of every tree of the garden you may freely eat; but of the tree of the knowledge of good and evil you shall not eat, for in the day that you eat of it you shall surely die."

(Bible, Torah, Genesis 2:16-17) God's warning was clear: disobedience leads to death.

God wanted them to live forever worshipping Him. God gave them a precious gift: free will! He did not make them like robots so that they would have to love and obey Him. Love must come freely. This gift of free will was one of the main differences between mankind and the animals. Adam and Eve could choose between right and wrong, good and bad. They could choose to do what God wanted or what they wanted, to live for God or for themselves.

They chose to disobey God! They preferred to please themselves rather than God.

Why did they do this? What went wrong?

It was the devil, Satan (شيطان - a name which means "the deceiver"), who tempted the first man and woman to choose wrong and disobey God. Adam and Eve ignored God's warning. The consequence? Death – spiritual and physical, as God had warned. "The wages of sin is death," is the way the Bible expresses it (Bible, Injil, Romans 6:23). Adam and Eve immediately died spiritually when they disobeyed.

What did spiritual death mean? It meant that their personal relationship with God was now broken because of their sin. Then, they were expelled from the Garden of Eden, the place where God was present in a special way. The expulsion from the garden illustrates the reality of their relationship with God being broken. It is because Adam died spiritually that he died physically several hundred years later. Adam and Eve would not have died if they had not disobeyed God. We see here the holiness of God and His moral obligation to condemn those who sin against Him. He cannot tolerate one single sin. Nor will He change what He has once declared.

Was Adam's sin just an accident?

No! Was it just ignorance? Was it just forgetfulness? Not at all! It was a deliberate choice to believe Satan's lie. It was disbelieving God and reckoning himself to be perfectly capable of looking after himself and going his own way. And that is the mind-set of every human being born into this world since Adam.

Suppose God said to a gardener, "I want you to trim these bushes by three o'clock this afternoon. But be careful. There is a large open pit at the edge of the garden. If you fall into that pit, you will not be able to get yourself out. So whatever you do, stay away from that pit." Suppose that as soon as God leaves the gardener runs over and jumps into the pit. At three o'clock God returns and finds the bushes untrimmed. He calls for the gardener and hears a faint cry from the edge of the garden. He walks to the edge of the pit and sees him helplessly flailing around on the bottom. He says, "Why haven't you trimmed the bushes as I asked you?" The gardener replies angrily, "How do you expect me to trim the bushes when I am trapped in this pit? If you hadn't left this empty pit here, I would not be in this predicament."

Adam's sin was not an accident or an act of ignorance. Adam didn't simply slip into sin; he jumped deliberately into it with both feet. He jumped into the pit. Adam was clearly warned about it. God had told him to stay away. The consequences Adam experienced from being in the pit were a direct punishment for jumping deliberately into it.

Was Adam's sin forgiven?

I know that Muslims believe that Adam and Eve sinned against God, but that they afterwards repented and that their repentance was accepted – with the effect that everything came back to normal again, and the divine plan prescribed for Adam and Eve took its due course.

If that was the case, my friend, why were they punished? Why were they left to die? All Muslims accept that Adam and Eve were driven out of the Garden when they sinned. If Adam and Eve were forgiven and things returned to normal, why weren't they allowed back into the Garden? They were never permitted to re-enter, nor has any subsequent member of the human race entered.

So I'd like to ask you: Why were you and I not born in paradise? Why do we die? Please read on to see the answer given in the holy Scriptures.

Adam - a federal headship!

The holy Scriptures tell us that when God first created the universe, He appointed one man to represent us in the Garden of

Eden (جنة عدن). The Hebrew name "Adam" means mankind. Adam was God's perfect choice for you and me. Just as a federal government has a chief spokesman, or representative, who is the head of the nation, so Adam was the federal head of mankind. My relationship with God depends on my representative's relationship with God. And so when Adam disobeyed, all mankind disobeyed! Sin (like poison) entered into our world and into human life.

Think of it like a set of dominoes. You can stand them all up in a long line. But if the first one falls down, what will happen to the rest? They will all fall too. In the same way, when the first man fell, all the rest of mankind fell too. Adam's fall was our fall. This is what Christians mean by "the inheritance of original sin". When God punished Adam by causing him to die, we were all likewise punished – we all die too. The curse of the fall affects us all.

The Hadith on the concept of the inheritance of Adam's sin

Again, for Christians the Qur'an and Hadith are not authoritative but, since Muslims draw their beliefs from these two sources I would like to remind them that the concept of the inheritance of original sin is obviously present in the Hadith in which Adam explicitly bears responsibility for humanity's exile from paradise: "Allah's apostle [Muhammad] said, 'Adam and Moses met, and Moses said to Adam, "You are the one who made people miserable and turned them out of Paradise."'" (Hadith, Bukhari, vol. 6, book 65, no. 4736). This clearly teaches that the human race somehow shares in Adam's exile.

Is it fair?

What have we seen so far? The consequence of Adam's sin was death. Any serious thinker should come to the same conclusion. But if we look at Adam's offspring (including ourselves) we find them suffering the same punishment of death as well. We are therefore faced with one of two conclusions:

1. Adam represented his descendants, in which case it is fair and just for his descendants to receive part of the punishment..., or,

2. Adam did not represent his descendants, in which case the infliction of punishment for sin on those who had no part in his fall is a great evil and manifest injustice – and God Himself is unjust!

Let me put it simply. If I have nothing to do with Adam's sin, then why should I share the consequence of his sin? Why wasn't I born in paradise? If I was born perfect (as Muslims believe), then, to be fair, God should have created me in paradise (as He did with Adam) and waited to see if I would disobey like Adam and Eve did. But He didn't, did He? I wasn't born in paradise!

The truth is that, as a result of what happened in the Garden of Eden, each of us are born with an insurmountable gap between us and God. We have all inherited Adam's sin. This is why we were not born in paradise. The prophet David wrote, "Behold, I was brought forth in iniquity, and in sin my mother conceived me" (Bible, Psalm 51:5). This is very true! Think about children. One of the first words little children pronounce is "no"! We all know their very early disobedience. Does anyone teach them how to be naughty? Do you think children need to be taught how to disobey? Of course not! Parents teach them good behaviour, but no-one needs to teach them naughtiness. By nature they know how to be naughty! It's in them from birth. What the prophet David said is absolutely true – we are born in iniquity, and in sin our mothers conceived us!

God is holy and we are sinful, so we are cut off from Him. A prophet said, "Your iniquities have separated you from your God, and your sins have hidden His face from you." (Bible, Isaiah 59:2)

To sum it up we could say that you and I are justly due for the same punishment as Adam because we are as disobedient and fallen as he was!

What is the solution?

It is God's solution! People want to have their own solutions, but we should always and only look at the solution that God has provided.

So much for the bad news about man: now for the good news. What did God do when Adam and Eve disobeyed? Did He destroy them? He could have done so. Did He say to them, "If you want to return to paradise then you must do more good deeds (حسنات)

than bad deeds (سيآت)"? No, no! No amount of good deeds could cancel out their sin.

So what was God's remedy for sin and its consequence, death? We read in the Torah that after Adam and Eve sinned God gave a promise:

> "So the Lord God said to the serpent: 'Because you have done this, you are cursed more than all cattle, and more than every beast of the field; on your belly you shall go, and you shall eat dust all the days of your life. And I will put enmity between you and the woman, and between your seed and her Seed; He shall bruise your head, and you shall bruise His heel.'" (Bible, Torah, Genesis 3:14-15)

Thank God that we find not only His holiness displayed here, but also His mercy. God's words to Satan are called "the first good news." What does God promise here? He promises a redeemer or deliverer – the seed of the woman (who is called "He"). This is a prophecy of a virgin birth. Notice that He doesn't say the seed of the man and the woman, but the seed of the woman, full stop. In other words, God said, "I am a holy God. I don't tolerate sin. I told you that the consequence of sin is death. I cannot just ignore sin. I must deal with it. There is only one remedy for sin and death. It is through what a Person will one day do. This Person will not have a human father. He will come only from a woman."

Now my dear friend, tell me: Who do you know in all of human history who was born only of a woman? Who, in all of human history, never had a human father? Yes, you have the right answer - only Jesus Christ! He was conceived by the Holy Spirit in Mary's womb. He is the fulfilment of God's promise here.

What would this promised deliverer do?

"I will put enmity between you [Satan] and the woman, and between your seed and her Seed; He shall bruise your head, and you shall bruise His heel." This is a prophecy concerning the suffering, death and victory of the seed of the woman over Satan. The power of Satan will be crushed through the seed of the woman. How will this happen? It will involve death!

Remember, "The wages of sin is death." So death is man's big problem. How could Jesus Christ deliver us without paying the full penalty for our sin? If anyone were to save us, he would have to solve this problem. He would have to conquer death – the very consequence of our sin. He would have to restore our broken relationship with God.

This is something you and I could never have done for ourselves or for others. God in His kindness says that the way we are to be saved is for Jesus Christ – the seed of the woman – to take death, spiritual and physical (which we deserve), upon Himself in our place.

The prophet Abraham

One day, God told Abraham to go up into the mountain and to sacrifice his son. When they arrived at the place of sacrifice his son asked him where the lamb for the sacrifice was. Abraham told him that God would supply the lamb. Then he tied his son to the altar. When he was ready to sacrifice him, the angel of the Lord called out to him and told him to stop. Abraham looked and saw a ram caught in the thicket. He took this ram and sacrificed it to the Lord. God had provided a substitute to take the place of the son that was to die. The ram died and the son lived. This is a picture of the death of Jesus. God sent Him as a substitute to take the place of the condemned. That is why when John the Baptist saw Jesus coming towards him he said of Him: "Behold! The Lamb of God, who takes away the sin of the world!" (Bible, Injil, John 1:29)

The Viking king

The story is told of a Viking king. In his kingdom everything went well: no stealing, no killing, everybody was happy. Then one day (imagine!) a theft took place in the treasury – a significant theft! They had never seen anything like it. Who could have done it? They searched high and low but could not find the thief; meanwhile more and more thefts occurred. The king decreed that every effort should be made to arrest the thief and that the punishment would be death by lashing. One day they found the thief. Do you know who it was? The mother of the king! What would the king do now? On the one hand he loved his mother; on the other hand he was a just king, obliged to punish her since he'd decreed the punishment publically. The big day arrived. The central arena was full of people. The whole city was there to see what the king would do. The king was there with his crown and kingly robe. His mother was then brought and tied up, ready to be whipped to death. Big silence! Everybody wondered what the king would do. Would he give the order to execute his own mother? Suddenly the king did the most incredible thing. He stood up, removed his crown, took off his robe and walked down the steps from the throne. He walked towards his mother, put his arms around her and covered her with his own body. Then he gave the order to the executioner: "Whip me!" The executioner whipped the king until the king died. His mother was left alive and free. Why? Because the king took her place. He bore her condemnation.

This is exactly what God has done for sinners. He cannot change what He has decreed: 'The wages of sin is death.' What would God do then to save sinners? The King of kings came down to earth in the Person of Jesus Christ. He says, "I want to save you. I want to take the punishment in your place. I want to bear the wages of your sin; I want to die so that you may live." The prophet Isaiah put it like this:

"Surely He has borne our griefs and carried our sorrows. Yet we esteemed Him stricken, smitten by God, and afflicted. But He was wounded for our transgressions. He was bruised for our iniquities; The chastisement for our peace was upon Him, and by His stripes we are healed. All we like sheep have gone astray. We have turned, every one, to his own way; and the LORD has laid on Him the iniquity of us all. ... For He was cut off from the land of the living. For the transgressions of My people He was stricken. ... Because He poured out His soul unto death, and He was numbered with the transgressors, and He bore the sin of many, and made intercession for the transgressors." (Bible, Isaiah 53:4-12)

Could the Viking king's love for his thieving mother be greater than God's love for people He created? No! "This is how we know what love is: Jesus Christ laid down His life for us." (Bible, Injil, 1 John 3:16) "Greater love has no one than this, than to lay down one's life for his friends." (Bible, Injil, John 15:13)

If Jesus didn't die then He wouldn't be the Saviour because the consequence of my sin and your sin –death – wouldn't have been solved. Without Jesus' death there would have been no way for us to escape God's punishment for our sin.

The first Adam and the last Adam

Here is how the Bible (Injil) summarizes what has been said in this booklet...

"Just as through one man [Adam] sin entered the world, and death through sin, and thus death spread to all men, because all sinned ... But the free gift *is* not like the offence. For if by the one man's [Adam's] offence many died, much more the grace of God and the gift by the grace of the one Man, Jesus Christ, abounded to many. ... For if by the one man's [Adam's] offence death reigned through the one [Adam], much more those who receive abundance of grace and of the gift of righteousness will reign in life through the One, Jesus Christ. Therefore, as through one man's [Adam's] offence judgment came to all men, resulting in condemnation, even so through one Man's [Christ's] righteous act the free gift came to all men, resulting in justification of life. For as by one man's [Adam's] disobedience many were made sinners, so also by one Man's [Christ's] obedience many will be made righteous." (Bible, Injil, Romans 5:12-20. Italics added)

Chapter 14

What is the evidence that Jesus defeated death?

How do we know that Jesus defeated death? The evidence is His resurrection from the dead. By raising Jesus from the dead, God declared to the world that He had accepted Jesus' sacrifice on our behalf.

The resurrection shows that death could not keep its hold on Jesus. It shows that God, the Judge, considered our penalty to have been paid. Our sins had been dealt with.

Anyone who has said goodbye at the graveside to a loved one who has died knows that death is a formidable enemy. Yet, for Christians facing death, there is the certainty of eternal life beyond the grave. This certainty comes from the knowledge that Jesus Christ overcame death. Jesus did this through His triumphant resurrection. "Death is swallowed up in victory. O Death, where is your sting?" (Bible, Injil, 1 Corinthians 15:54-55)

Therefore, because Jesus has conquered death, He can raise those who put their trust in Him from spiritual death. In other words, He saves them. He gives them a new heart and eternal life. God will no longer frown on them because their sins have been dealt with by Jesus. The punishment they deserve (God's wrath and eternal death in hell) was taken by Jesus. Because Jesus conquered death, one day there will also be a Day of Resurrection, a Day of Judgment when all the dead will rise, and all humanity will stand before God to be judged. However, for those who trust in Christ, that day will be a day of reward – not because of their own goodness, but only because they trusted in what Jesus did for them. Jesus says to all who trust Him:

"Let not your heart be troubled; you believe in God, believe also in Me. In My Father's house are many mansions; if it were not so, I would have told you. I go to prepare a place for you. And if I go and prepare a place for you, I will come again and receive you to Myself; that where I am, there you may be also. And where I go you know, and the way you know." (Bible, Injil, John 14:1-4)

The passage continues,

"Thomas said to Him, 'Lord, we do not know where You are going, and how can we know the way?' Jesus said to him, 'I am the way, the truth, and the life. No one comes to the Father except through Me.'" (Bible, Injil, John 14:5-6).

Conclusion

For a person to know the truth, it is essential for him to have a sincere, heart-felt desire for it, and a determination to accept the truth, no matter how much it will cost him. Christ says, "You shall know the truth, and the truth shall make you free" (Bible, Injil, John 8:32). God is always willing to reveal the truth to the sincere seeker, to the one who perseveres in asking God for it.

Jesus really died! Does that mean that He was defeated by those evil people? No! The New Testament (Injil) explains that it was not out of weakness that God allowed Jesus to be crucified. Jesus said, "I lay down My life that I may take it again. No one takes it from Me, but I lay it down of Myself. I have power to lay it down, and I have power to take it again." (Bible, Injil, John 10:17-18) Yes, Christ could have saved Himself if He had wanted. But we saw that He came to give His life as a ransom for many. That is, He came to die on behalf of those who would put their trust in Him. When Judas came with the soldiers to arrest Him, He told His disciple who wanted to defend Him with the sword, that in a moment He could have summoned a legion of angels to rescue Him and destroy these evil people, "But how then could the Scriptures be fulfilled, that it must happen thus?" (Bible, Injil,

Matthew 26:53-54) He chose to die because He knew that only through His death could God's plan to save sinners be accomplished.

Christ announced from heaven, "I am He who lives, and was dead, and behold, I am alive forevermore. Amen." (Bible, Injil, Revelation 1:18)

My prayer is that God will be glorified and that you would benefit as you read this booklet. I give praise to our loving, holy, just, gracious and merciful God of whom this booklet endeavours to speak. God alone is worthy, and so to Him be all praise and worship, both now and forever!

E.M. Hicham

Quiz

If you have read this booklet carefully, you should be able to answer the following questions. These questions are arranged in the order of the chapters. I encourage you to re-read each corresponding chapter before you make your responses. We would love to see your answers. So why not send them to us at the following address:

> Word of Hope Ministries,
> PO Box 24,
> Rochdale,
> OL16 3FB, UK

Introduction

1. Why do Muslims deny Christ's crucifixion?

2. How would you respond to the statement: "God would never have allowed His prophet Jesus to die in a horrible way"?

Chapter 1: What did the prophets before Jesus say?

1. Is the death of Jesus an idea that Christians invented in the first century?

2. Can you name some of the prophets who lived before Jesus and foretold the death of the coming Messiah?

3. What is so amazing about the prophecy of Isaiah 53?

4. Why do you think the Jews do not include Isaiah 53 in their religious readings these days?

5. The Jews kept this chapter in their Holy Scriptures (Tawrat, Zabur, and Prophetic Writings). What does this prove concerning the truthfulness and trustworthiness of the Bible?

Chapter 2: What did Jesus Himself say?

1. How would you respond to the statement: "Jesus never said that He would die"?

2. According to Matthew 20:28, why did Jesus come to the world?

Chapter 3: What did the apostles of Jesus say?

1. Did the apostles change the content of their message concerning Jesus' death?

2. A great many people who had witnessed Jesus' execution were still living when the apostles preached Jesus' death. Did anyone challenge the apostles' claims? What does that prove?

Chapter 4: What did the Roman authorities say?

1. How did the Roman authorities certify the death of Jesus?

Chapter 5: What did the medical testimony say?

1. What do you think of the "swoon theory" taught by Ahmadiyya Muslims, Ahmad Deedat and Zakir Naik?

2. In the crucifixion story it is stated that a spear was thrust into Jesus' side under His heart in order to make sure that He was dead. Blood and water came out. Medically, what does that prove?

Chapter 6: What did early Christians say?
1. Why is the witness of the early church fathers important?

Chapter 7: What do the practices of early Christians say?
1. Does archaeology support the death of Jesus? Can you give an example?

2. What do the two ordinances of the Lord's Supper and Baptism symbolize?

3. What does the practice of these ordinances by both first century Christians and all Christians throughout the ages prove concerning the death of Jesus?

Chapter 8: What did secular historians say?
1. What can be learned from the references to Christ's death in secular documents?

Chapter 9: What does the Qur'an say?
1. What are the various ways of interpreting Surah 4:157-158

2. What does the parallel between Surah Maryam 19:33 and Surah Maryam 19:15 show?

3. What is the meaning of mutawaffika as it is used in Surah Al-Imran 3:55 and Surah Al-Maida 5:116-117?

Chapter 10: What do many Islamic scholars say?
1. Do all Islamic scholars agree on the interpretation of the

Qur'anic passages which speak about the death of Jesus?

2. Can you name some of the well respected Islamic scholars who taught that Jesus died a physical death?

3. What should you conclude from the extensive contradiction and confusion in what Muslim scholars have to say about the death of Christ?

Chapter 11: Did someone else die in Jesus' place?

1. Is the Muslim theory of substitution supported by any historical proof?

2. How would the Muslim theory of substitution blacken the character of God?

3. Why is the claim that Judas Iscariot died in Jesus' place erroneous?

4. How does Jesus' behaviour before His death contrast with Judas' behaviour?

5. How does the case of Jesus' body support the death of Jesus?

6. What other argument did the author use to show that it would have been impossible for someone else to die in Jesus' place?

7. Contrast a God who deliberately allowed His people to believe a lie for over 600 years with a God who keeps His promises and stands by His Word. Who would you rather trust and serve?

Chapter 12: So, did Jesus really die?

1. Can you summarize the evidence that Christ died on the cross?

Chapter 13: Why was Jesus' death necessary anyway?

1. Why is it important to understand what happened in the Garden of Eden in order to understand why Jesus came?

2. What was God's original creation like?

3. On what condition did God say that man could stay in the Garden of Eden?

4. What did Adam and Eve do wrong?

5. What were the consequences?

6. Muslims believe that Adam and Eve sinned against God, but that they afterwards repented and that their repentance was accepted – with the effect that everything returned to normal. After reading pages 43 to 49, what would your reply be?

7. What does it mean for Adam to be a federal head?

8. Do people today experience the same consequences of sin as Adam and Eve did? In what way?

9. What was God's remedy for man's sinful nature?

10. God's promise in Genesis 3:14-15 is about the seed of the woman. How did Jesus fulfill this promise?

11. Can you summarize the parallels between what Adam and Jesus did?

12. What is the parallel between the ram that was sacrificed in the place of Abraham's son, and Jesus' death?

Chapter 14: What is the evidence that Jesus defeated death?

1. What is the evidence that Jesus defeated death?

2. What else does Jesus' resurrection prove in terms of salvation?

3. How do Christians view death and why?

Conclusion

4. Jesus really died! Does that mean that He was defeated by those evil people? Was it out of weakness?

5. After studying this booklet, the question you are left with is: What does Jesus' death mean to you personally?

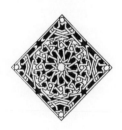

If you would like to receive further information,
please contact us.

If you wish to make further study of the
Christian faith correspondence courses
in English, Arabic and French are available from:

Word of Hope Ministries
PO Box 24,
Rochdale,
OL16 3FB,
England

Email: **contact@word-of-hope.net**
Web: **www.word-of-hope.net**

Do you speak French?
www.Jesus-Islam.fr